Fallschirmjäger

IMAGES OF WAR

Fallschirmjäger

Elite German Paratroops in World War II

Rare Photographs from Wartime Archives

Jon Sutherland
and Diane Canwell

Pen & Sword
AVIATION

First published in Great Britain in 2010 by
PEN & SWORD AVIATION
An imprint of
Pen & Sword Books Ltd
47 Church Street
Barnsley
South Yorkshire
S70 2AS

Copyright © Jon Sutherland and Diane Canwell, 2010

ISBN 978 1 84884 318 9

A CIP catalogue record for this book is
available from the British Library

Typeset by Phoenix Typesetting, Auldgirth, Dumfriesshire
Printed and bound in Great Britain by CPI UK

Pen & Sword Books Ltd incorporates the imprints of
Pen & Sword Aviation, Pen & Sword Family History, Pen & Sword Maritime,
Pen & Sword Military, Wharncliffe Local History, Pen & Sword Select,
Pen & Sword Military Classics, Leo Cooper, Remember When, Seaforth Publishing
and Frontline Publishing

For a complete list of Pen & Sword titles please contact
PEN & SWORD BOOKS LIMITED
47 Church Street, Barnsley, South Yorkshire, S70 2AS, England
E-mail: enquiries@pen-and-sword.co.uk
Website: www.pen-and-sword.co.uk

Contents

Introduction

The photographs in this collection belonged to First Sergeant Wilhelm Plieschen, who served with the 2nd Company of the Fallschirm-Maschinengewehr-Battalion, as part of the 7th *Flieger* Division. The album is in three parts; the first charts the progress of the unit through the Balkans, taking the men from Austria, through Romania and Bulgaria, and into Greece. Although the men at the time did not know it they were destined to be airlifted to Crete. Indeed, Plieschen would find himself involved in the German attempt to seize Rethymno on 20 May 1941. It was to be a desperate and dangerous experience and many of his fellow paratroopers would be killed. The album then moves from Crete to the early experiences in Russia, probably in 1942.

The Germans had used their airborne soldiers or *Fallschirmjäger* on attacks in the west in 1940. They had been utilised against Denmark, Norway, Belgium and Holland. Perhaps the most stunning exploit was the capture of the Belgian fort Eben Emael with a garrison of 1,200 men with heavy weapons, artillery and anti-aircraft guns – all silenced by sixty-eight German *Fallschirmjäger*.

At the beginning of the war the Germans were aware of the potential of either parachute or glider-borne troops. It had been glider-borne men that had seized the Belgian fortress. Paratroopers were used to take airfields and bridges across Holland.

Not all of the assaults were successful; they were often risky operations. Everything relied on securing a drop zone and breaking out from it after securing a suitable landing zone for reinforcement. The Germans had seen a notable success in Norway, at Narvik. Some of the drop zones had been easily overrun, but in other cases the British forces had simply withdrawn from the area.

By the time that it was Holland's turn to feel the brunt of the German offensive it was clear that there were many objectives across the country that needed to be seized ahead of ground forces. Several bridges and airfields were earmarked and the *Fallschirmjäger* was also charged with the task of trying to capture the Dutch royal family. An important lesson was not learned by the Germans in this operation; although many of the objectives were seized relatively quickly, fierce counter-attacks from Dutch troops proved that the *Fallschirmjäger* would struggle to hold onto the gains unless reinforced. One of the key problems was the lack of heavy weapons.

By 1941 the *Fallschirmjäger* was recognised as being a potential key to tricky operations. Much to the annoyance of the Germans they had become embroiled in the Balkans. Mussolini, irritated and somewhat ashamed of the German successes in the west, perversely chose to attack Greece, although his army was in no fit state to launch such an operation. The net result saw the Greeks throwing the Italians back over the Albanian border and threatening to overrun the hard-pressed Italians. With German plans to launch a major offensive against Russia, they found themselves pulled into a situation that needed to be resolved with the maximum speed. Having attacked Greece the Italians had given the British ample opportunity to reinforce the mainland. Germany could not countenance British bombers being in range of their newly acquired Romanian oilfields. Consequently, not only did the Greeks have to be overrun, but the British also had to be ejected from the Greek mainland.

German troops poured across the Greek borders and Greek and Commonwealth forces began to slowly retreat. Hitler authorised the launching of Operation *Hannibal* on 26 April 1941. *Fallschirmjäger* would seize the bridge at Corinth and cut off the retreating enemy and prevent their evacuation. The bridge carried the only road that crossed the Corinth Canal, linking mainland Greece with the Peloponnese Peninsula. *Fallschirmjäger* pioneers landed in gliders close to the bridge and immediately began to remove demolition charges. The bridge was partially destroyed during a counter-attack, but by then many more *Fallschirmjäger* had been dropped and they could secure the bridge area. As a result, 12,000 Commonwealth and Greek troops were cut off and captured, for the loss of sixty-three *Fallschirmjäger* killed.

An even more ambitious operation was to be launched less than a month later. Once again the Germans recognised that the Mediterranean would continue to be under threat from Commonwealth forces as long as Crete remained un-occupied. The entire 7th *Flieger* Division of four regiments plus pioneers of paratroopers, the *Luftlande Sturm* Regiment of four battalions (glider troops) supported by the 5th Mountain Division, would be launched at the Greek island. Glider troops would land on the west of the island, around the airfield of Maleme. Later, air-dropped units and German mountain troops would support them once drop zones and landing fields had been seized. More troops would drop around Chania, the former capital of the island. Additional troops would target the other two major centres of population on the island – Rethymno and the new capital, Heraklion.

What the Germans did not know was that their top-secret communications had been intercepted by Ultra. The operation was difficult enough, but this was compounded by the fact that the Germans lacked enough transport aircraft to make one decisive airlift. This meant that the troops being landed around Maleme and Chania would have to bear the brunt of all counter-attacks until the aircraft flew back to their bases, refuelled and then dropped the second wave of troops around Rethymno and Heraklion in the afternoon. Some of the drops were delayed and some of the drop zones were changed, but one of the major problems was that many of the *Fallschirmjäger* were scattered across the countryside.

The *Fallschirmjäger* faced mainly dispirited and poorly equipped British and Commonwealth troops. The handful of depleted Greek regiments on the island only had a smattering of rifles and virtually no ammunition. Nonetheless, a spirited and nearly decisive defence was put up, primarily by the New Zealanders, as well as some British units and Cretan irregulars. The Germans were very lucky in being able to take control of Maleme airfield; it was the key to winning the battle for the island. With the airfield open to German air traffic and reinforcement, the battle of Crete was as good as lost for the Allies.

Fallschirmjäger casualties were ruinous; over 1,900 were killed, nearly 1,800 were missing and over 1,600 were wounded. From this point on Hitler would not countenance deploying *Fallschirmjäger* in such an offensive role ever again. Henceforth they would be elite ground troops.

Plieschen's unit was later deployed to Russia but in later years the Western Allies would run up against German airborne troops in a ground role at Monte Cassino, in Normandy and in Holland.

We are indebted to James Payne for the use of the photographs. Readers may be interested to know that they can purchase their own high resolution scans on CD of the images via his website – www.throughtheireyes2.co.uk.

Chapter One

Through the Balkans

The *Fallschirmjäger's* equipment and uniforms were extremely distinctive. Effectively, they would wear a jump smock, designed to prevent them from getting entangled in the glider or aircraft or when trying to open their parachutes. Most of the photographs show the *Fallschirmjäger* in the first pattern jump smock. It was produced in either a light green or grey cotton. The paratrooper would step into the garment and then push his arms through the sleeves. They were buttoned from the front. There were various versions, particularly with the number of pockets and their position.

A *Fallschirmjäger's* steel helmet was of a revolutionary design. It had to fulfil three purposes; it was almost rimless, it needed to give a degree of protection in combat, protect the head in difficult landings and also not to snag either the parachute or rigging. It was normal practice for the helmet to be finished in a field blue colour, but there were a number of different colours actually used and, as we will see, by the time the paratroopers were operating in Russia, they would whitewash the helmets for additional camouflage.

The *Fallschirmjäger* also had ammunition bandoliers and pouches. The bandoliers were unique to the *Fallschirmjäger*. The men needed to be as self-sufficient as possible and carry as much of their own ammunition as was practicable. The bandoliers consisted of two rows of ten pouches; each of the pouches carried a clip of five rounds for their rifles. The bandolier was worn around the neck and held in place by loops of cloth. The jump trousers were woollen and had a special knife pocket. Early jump boots had laces up one side; later ones were front-laced.

Each of the *Fallschirmjäger* carried a sidearm. One of the principal problems was that the paratroopers landed just armed with the knife, a sidearm and grenades. They had to find the weapons containers, which had floated down on a parachute from the same aircraft. This meant that the men were able to protect themselves and, as in Crete, actually mount attacks just armed with a pistol and grenades. The primary weapon was the Mauser K98, which had a rate of fire of fifteen rounds a minute. Only a handful of the men at this stage of the war were armed with a machine pistol. Plieschen, as a member of the machine gun company, would have been well versed in the use of the MG34. It was a general-purpose squad machine gun and could be fired on a bipod, which was usually attached, or a tripod for continuous fire. This also meant that the members of his company would be expected to carry a great deal of MG34 ammunition. The MG34 had a maximum range of some 800 metres and had a theoretical rate of fire of 1,200 rounds per minute. The men would use a fifty-round belt.

Wilhelm Plieschen's unit was commanded by *Hauptmann* Erich Schulz, who had joined the company in June 1940 and was later to be promoted to the rank of major. It is believed that Schulz was either badly injured or wounded on Crete in the first few days. The parent unit of Plieschen's company was the 7th *Flieger* Division, which had been formed in 1938. Some elements of the division had operated as motorised infantry in Poland. As we have already seen, other parts of the division were active in Denmark, Norway, Belgium and the Netherlands. The division was also earmarked for the planned invasion of Britain in the summer of 1940.

It had been the 2nd Regiment of the division that had landed around the Corinth Canal. Initially, the division had been commanded by Kurt Student, who had been a fighter pilot in the First World War. By January 1941 Student had become the commanding general of the 11th *Fliegerkorps* and so, in this role, it was he that masterminded Operation *Mercury*. Over a year later Student also outlined Operation *Hercules*, which was the planned airborne invasion of Malta, but this was never carried out. By the time Plieschen found himself in Crete the new commander of his division was Major General Wilhelm Sussmann, although he was killed *en route* to Crete on 20 May 1941. The tow rope pulling his glider snapped and the glider crashed on the island of Aegina. Divisional command passed to Major Alfred Sturm.

The first third of the album shows the *Fallschirmjäger* in transit from their training base in Austria and their travels through the Balkans to their ultimate destination, Greek airfields on the mainland. Back in January 1936 the Germans had set up their first parachute training school at the *Luftwaffe* base at Stendal, some ninety-six kilometres to the west of Berlin. The training programme called for new recruits to spend eight weeks toughening themselves up in order to fulfil essentially a light infantry role. Here, the men would undergo physical exercises, drilling, bayonet practice, unarmed combat and weapons instruction. Many of the men had already received instruction on the use of grenades and the rifle. They were now introduced to pistols, sub-machine guns, machine guns, mines and mortars. They were also lectured on tactics at squad level and would be involved in field exercises up to battalion level. The idea was to build them into a team, but a flexible one that would be able to cope with a variety of challenging operations.

Once the basic training had been concluded the men then underwent a sixteen-day parachute course. Initially, they were shown how to execute high jumps on trampolines, or by somersaulting. It was important for the men to learn how to land properly and without breaking their bones.

Unlike Allied paratroopers, the German *Fallschirmjäger* was taught how to pack their own parachutes. Usually the parachutes were suspended from rails in an aircraft hangar. This was to ensure that there were no tears or faults and that the parachutes were kept dry. They were then laid out onto long tables. Two men would learn the pattern in which the parachute had to be folded in order for it to not only open, but also to fit into the pack. The parachutes of the *Fallschirmjäger* opened using static lines. This allowed the men to be dropped from lower heights. The canopies were 8.5 metres in diameter. They were packed into cloth bags and then the bag and the top of the folded canopy were fixed to a 9-metre static line. This would ensure that the parachute was fully deployed before the paratrooper had dropped 30 metres. It was a flexible system and allowed drops from as little as 100 metres.

Each of the recruits, in order to win their *Fallschirmschützenabzeichen*, or parachutist badge, had to complete six drops. They were given knee pads to prevent injury. Once on board the Ju52 aircraft the men held the end of their static lines between their teeth so that their hands were free. The dispatcher, or *absetze*, effectively the instructor at this stage, would have checked the harness and pack and once the aircraft had reached a suitable height he would order the men to stand up and hook their static lines to a cable that ran the length of the aircraft. The first *Fallschirmjäger* in the stick (or group of men) would be told to stand near the doorway. The paratrooper would then launch himself out of the aircraft in a spreadeagle position. The parachute would deploy after a short drop. When the man hit the ground he would roll and then grab the shroud lines and try to deflate the parachute. If necessary he would use his combat knife to cut himself free.

Each of the recruits would be required to drop five more times, in different conditions, although at this early stage in the war night drops were not practised. At this point the qualified *Fallschirmjäger*, proudly wearing his badge, would then be sent to his battalion and be ready for active duty.

Plieschen is pictured on the left. This photograph was probably taken at the parachute training school. By this stage other training centres had been set up and this one may have been in Austria. The two men are wearing their jump smocks and unique *Fallschirmjäger* helmets. They are wearing first-pattern jump smocks and standard combat trousers tucked into side-laced jump boots. Plieschen wears a Luger holster. The insignia worn on the jump smock is of a *Luftwaffe* eagle. Rank insignia would have been worn on both upper arms. Normally, medals and decorations were not permitted, but later the men would have had cuff titles, such as Kreta (Crete). Note that neither of these men yet has the coveted parachutist badge, which may suggest that they were still in training. They wear black leather gauntlets and in battle they would have carried ammunition boxes attached to the waist belt, a water bottle and drinking cup on the right hip. These early issue helmets were blue/grey. The German national colours of black, white and red were worn on the right and the silver grey *Luftwaffe* eagle on the left. It is not possible to see whether the national colours are on these men's helmets, but they were removed early on in the war.

The coveted *Luftwaffe* parachutist's badge is shown here. During the war years training for this parachute qualification was carried out at regimental training schools. The recruits would have four weeks of ground training and four weeks of airborne training. The volunteers had to be relatively lightweight; around 85 kg. They could not have any fear of heights, or suffer from dizziness or air sickness. Throughout the training programme initiative, intelligence and courage were looked for from the recruits. It was an arduous training programme and it was of course different for paratroopers and glider units. The men were issued with the so-called parachutists' Ten Commandments:

1. You are the elite of the German army. For you, combat shall be fulfilment. You shall seek it out and train yourself to stand any test.
2. Cultivate true comradeship, for together with your comrades you will triumph or die.
3. Be shy of speech and incorruptible. Men act, women chatter; chatter will bring you to the grave.
4. Calm and caution, vigour and determination, valour and a fanatical offensive spirit will make you superior in attack.
5. In facing the foe, ammunition is the most precious thing. He who shoots uselessly, merely to reassure himself, is a man without guts. He is a weakling and does not deserve the title of paratrooper.
6. Never surrender. Your honour lies in Victory or Death.
7. Only with good weapons can you have success. So look after them on the principle – first my weapons, then myself.
8. You must grasp the full meaning of an operation so that, should your leader fall by the way, you can carry it out with coolness and caution.
9. Fight chivalrously against an honest foe; armed irregulars deserve no quarter.
10. Keep your eyes wide open. Tune yourself to the top most pitch. Be nimble as a greyhound, as tough as leather, as hard as Krupp steel and so you shall be the German warrior incarnate.

Paratroopers entrained, probably in Austria. The situation in the Balkans prior to the Greeks entering the war had been complicated. German troops had entered Bulgaria in the spring of 1941. The Germans had set up supply points as close to the Greek border as possible, including some in Romania. Yugoslavia had been overrun in just twelve days and the armistice had been signed at 1200 hours on 18 April 1941. The German 2nd Parachute Regiment, reinforced by engineers, had seized the Corinth Canal on 26 April. In order to facilitate this attack 400 Ju52s and towing aircraft, along with troop and cargo-carrying gliders, had been shifted from Bulgaria to the former British airfield at Larisa. If the organisation necessary to carry out this relatively small attack had been complex then the massive troop, equipment and aircraft movement necessary to tackle Crete seemed insuperable.

A photograph taken from the window of the train as it passed through the mountainous areas of Austria. Note that it appears that the snow is still thick on the ground, indicating that this is a high region of Austria early in the journey into the Balkans.

The troop train moves slowly across a railway bridge, possibly in Bulgaria or Romania. The Germans would have to shift their entire parachute army to airfields in Greece and supporting aircraft to the Italian-held Dodecanese Islands. A German army division had actually been trained for air landings, but it could not be included in the invasion of Crete, as it was needed to guard the Romanian oilfields. As a result, this division's role was taken by the 5th Mountain Division. They had no practical experience of airborne work. This massive troop movement was as a result a compromise; 15,000 combat troops would either be brought in by glider or parachute onto the island and 7,000 more would be brought in by a ragtag collection of vessels.

This is a posed shot of *Fallschirmjäger* around a command vehicle. The men are wearing their field blouse uniforms, which were shorter than normal service tunics and popular with the *Fallschirmjäger*. The men are wearing standard field caps, or *feldmütze* (M40). There is a mix of ranks shown in the photograph; the single wing on the epaulette signifies a *jäger*, or private, two wings shows a *gefreiter* and three indicate an *obergefreiter*. A *gefreiter* was effectively a lance corporal and an *obergefreiter* was the equivalent of a senior lance corporal.

This is a broader view of the German troop train, either in Bulgaria or Romania. Note the flat cars with the trucks and to the rear of these it is possible to see smaller trucks and transports. The Germans encountered many obstacles as soon as they crossed the Greek border. The Greeks and the British had demolished sections of roads and bridges. Some of the craters along defiles were 100 feet in diameter. The Germans had swiftly extracted as many troops as possible out of Greece due to their impending invasion of Russia. This had actually been done before many of the Greek forces were completely disarmed and the area pacified.

Here we see the handing out of rations to the men and hopeful Bulgarian civilians. Tsar Boris of Bulgaria is quoted as having said 'My army is pro-German, my wife is Italian, my people are pro-Russian. I am the only pro-Bulgarian in the country'. Bulgaria was a small state trying to pursue its own self-interests. Bulgaria was to find itself in an impossible position as the war ended, as she had found herself simultaneously at war with Great Britain, Germany, Russia and the United States.

This dramatic photograph shows an extensive troop train carrying masses of trucks and other vehicles making its way through a valley. At this stage of the war the Germans would have had little to fear from partisans and enemy aircraft attacks. Hence, looking in detail at this photograph, it is difficult to see whether any anti-aircraft defences are in position. As the war drew on, armoured trains with twelve to eighteen railroad cars and an armoured locomotive with a coal tender would have been used. It would also have been protected by anti-aircraft guns and groups of soldiers would have been assigned to each train to carry out reconnaissance and to pursue any attackers. The Germans had used armoured trains in the war in Yugoslavia. They had already acquired several of these trains from Austria, Czechoslovakia and Poland.

A group of officers and men are chatting to a railroad worker. The 7th *Flieger* Division had left its barracks in Germany under heavy security. They were not told their destination but were instructed to remove all of their insignia and to travel as if they were ordinary *Luftwaffe* personnel. All of their parachute equipment was to be hidden away. An order by *Hauptmann* Shulz to Plieschen's *Fallschirmjäger* MG Battalion 7 stated:

No member of the battalion is to carry any personal papers or documents with him. Buying and sending postcards as well as using the civilian postal service is strictly forbidden. It is forbidden to sing *Fallschirmjäger* songs. Railway coaches as well as vehicles must bear no identification marks. The special markings identifying our battalion must disappear from all vehicles.

This is a female nurse and a woman from the *Luftwaffe* on the train. The vast majority of the 1,500-mile journey all the way to Athens was completed by rail, on board slow-moving troop trains. The division's 3,000 vehicles were offloaded in Romania and driven the remaining 500 miles. The troops began arriving between 8 and 12 May 1941. Despite all of the Germans' efforts to keep the troop movement a secret the British, in Egypt and on Crete, had been made aware of the situation within thirty-six hours, due to the cracked Enigma codes.

DISCOVER MORE ABOUT MILITARY HISTORY

Frontline Books is an imprint of Pen & Sword Books, which has more than 1500 titles in print covering all aspects of military history on land, sea and air. If you would like to receive more information and special offers on your preferred interests from time to time, along with our standard catalogue, please indicate your areas of interest below and return this card (no stamp required in the UK). Alternatively, register online at www.frontline-books.com. Thank you.

PLEASE NOTE: We do not sell data information to any third party companies

Mr/Mrs/Ms/Other................... Name..

Address...

.... Postcode.................................

Email address..
If you wish to receive our email newsletter, please tick here ☐

PLEASE SELECT YOUR AREAS OF INTEREST

Ancient History ☐	Medieval History ☐	English Civil War ☐
Napoleonic ☐	Pre World War One ☐	World War One ☐
World War Two ☐	Post World War Two ☐	Falklands ☐
Aviation ☐	Maritime ☐	Battlefield Guides ☐
Regimental History ☐	Military Reference ☐	Military Biography ☐

Website: www.frontline-books.com • Email: info@frontline-books.com
Telephone: 01226 734555 • Fax: 01226 734438

Frontline Books
FREEPOST SF5
47 Church Street
BARNSLEY
South Yorkshire
S70 2BR

This civilian appears to be a Greek peasant in traditional costume, or possibly a shepherd. As the *Fallschirmjäger* pressed south they passed German tank regiments on their way back north. The soldiers that they saw were burned brown by the sun and could not help taunting the *Luftwaffe* men that the fighting was over and they had missed out.

As this border guard is still armed, we must assume that he is Romanian. This area of the Balkans saw enormous troop movements in the spring of 1941. German troops that had been involved in the Greek campaign were moving *en masse* to the north to assemble for the intended invasion of Russia. Other second-line troops were arriving as part of the occupation force. The *Fallschirmjäger*, as far as the people in the Balkans were concerned, were just yet another German unit on the move. As the paratroopers approached Greece, rumour was rife as to the nature of their mission and despite all attempts to prevent gossip and rumours men began to draw their own conclusions.

A young, barefoot Greek peasant boy views the German troops with a mixture of fear and fascination. The Greek campaign had been a short and decisive one. The Germans had launched Operation *Marita* on 6 April 1941. They had thrust across the Yugoslavian and Bulgarian borders. Initially, they had run into stiff opposition. The main Greek and Allied defensive position, the Metaxas Line, had been fully compromised by 9 April. Thessaloniki had been taken and this led to the collapse of Greek resistance in that region. The Germans had pressed the withdrawing enemy troops, harrying them. The British tried to make a stand at Thermopolis, but this was overcome during the night of 24/25 April and then came the blow that seized the Corinth Canal bridge. The Germans drove, triumphantly, into Athens on 27 April.

A German truck makes its way along a road in Athens. When the Germans entered Athens on 27 April 1941 the streets were virtually empty. The government had fled for Crete. The streets had been subjected to enemy aircraft attack and many of the Athenians stubbornly shut up their homes and remained inside. The Germans hoisted their flag on the Acropolis and installed a puppet prime minister, the former General Georgios Tsolakoglou.

A *Fallschirmjäger* camp in Greece is shown here. One of the commanders of an air training battalion, Baron von der Heydte, said of the parachutists:

I like the adventurers best. They jumped easily into life and they found it worth living for, whatever it brought along, provided it did not become monotonous. Their heads were filled with nonsensical pranks but also with good ideas. You could go horse stealing with them, but you could also take them on any patrol. They were born parachutists. Many of them had committed some offence, only to become honest with us. Others had run away from home solely to prove themselves men.

This shows a celebratory parade. The women are probably Romanian, or Bulgarian. A large number of German military personnel are in the crowds. Bulgaria had tried to stay neutral, but it had much to gain by aligning itself with the Germans, as it was promised a port onto the Aegean Sea. Their alignment with Germany brought short-term benefits in the shape of the occupation of Thrace and Macedonia. This photograph may well have been taken in Macedonia, which had endured from their perspective a long period of domination from Belgrade. In Thrace the Bulgarians were somewhat ruthless in trying to eject resident Greeks, leading to an uprising in September 1941, which was violently suppressed.

This shows a Bulgarian peasant farmer and his daughter waving at passing German troops. The Bulgarians' elation with regard to the acquisition of new territories was short-lived, particularly after the Germans attacked Russia in June 1941, when there were Communist demonstrations. Bulgaria had signed a treaty with the Germans in March 1941, allowing them to use their naval facilities, airbases and railway lines.

The *Fallschirmjäger* unit takes a train break. Note the absence of *Fallschirmjäger* insignia, as ordered by Schulz. Whilst the troops were moving south German planners were feverishly working on getting all the necessary stores, equipment, aircraft and fuel into position. The Corinth Canal was blocked by the wreckage of the bridge and it was not open until 17 May 1941, after German naval divers had removed a sufficient amount of the wreckage for vessels to get through.

Most of the *Fallschirmjäger*'s uniform was standard *Luftwaffe*. In this picture we can see that the men wear a mixture of the tapered waist flying service blouse and the four-pocketed service tunic. All of the men have a holstered sidearm.

Two men from the unit in fatigue dress, sitting on the back of a German truck as it passes through a village. For some of the men the trip through the Balkans was not entirely by train, as many had to accompany the transports. Note that even the chalk numbers on the back of the truck have been rubbed off in an attempt to prevent any form of identification of the unit.

These are men from a motorcycle reconnaissance unit, or *Aufklarung*. During the Crete operation 95 *Aufklarung* Battalion was a part of the 5th *Gebirgsjäger* Division and designated as air landing reserves.

These trucks are moving through the Greek countryside. As far as the Germans were concerned the Greeks were a friendly nation and their civilisation was admired. Many of the Greeks did not cooperate with the German occupation force, but most chose passive acceptance. Large numbers of people fled into the countryside, where a thriving and effective partisan movement was set up. It is significant to see this unprotected German truck convoy moving along a road and therefore it must be very shortly after the Greek capitulation.

These are the truck born elements of the *Fallschirmjäger* units, whilst taking a break on waste ground in a Greek town. Note that in the tree line in the shade are large numbers of horses. In fact, until the very end of the war many German artillery units were still horse-drawn. In this early *Blitzkrieg* period German reconnaissance units would also be mounted.

An aerial view, presumably of the Greek mainland; note the mountains in the distance. This would give the *Fallschirmjäger* a taste of the kind of countryside in which they would be expected to fight in Crete. Beyond the plains on the coastline the hillsides are steep and cut with gulleys and dry water beds and rise into rocky terrain and then high mountains.

Another view of the lorry park in Greece. In terms of German planning, everything that the men would need would be parachuted down with them and heavier equipment would be brought in by aircraft once one of the airfields had been secured. Theoretically, a full German *Fallschirmjäger* battalion would have twice the fire power of a standard British infantry battalion. This meant shipping rifles, machine guns, mortars, grenades, light field guns and of course all of the ammunition that they would need. In addition, water containers, food and medical stores would also be parachuted in.

Here the *Fallschirmjäger* is taking a last break on the road, as they head towards the airfields in the south of the Greek mainland. Each of the parachute battalions had 550 men organised into four companies. A brigade group could be as many as 2,000 men. Each of the battalions of the storm regiments was 600 strong; these were the air landing troops. The battalion would need seventy gliders. The paratroopers, in their Ju52s, would be dropped in groups of twelve. They would need to carry enough rations of bread and chocolate, along with thirst-quenching tablets, cooking utensils, a blanket and a small water bottle, to last them for two days.

Here we see a close-up of some of the battalion transports. The smaller vehicles in the front are Horch field cars. These vehicles had V8 engines and were designed to carry six to eight passengers. They were extremely flexible vehicles and had been developed during the 1930s and continued in production until 1942, by which time over 10,000 had been made.

This may be one of the Greek ports, although it does not appear to be the main harbour near Athens, Piraeus. A key part of the operation against Crete would be to transport all of the heavy equipment, along with the bulk of the mountain division and some *Fallschirmjäger* for which there was no room on aircraft. This meant that the Germans had to scrape together whatever vessels fell into their hands. Many of them were simple fishing boats and others little more than barges. The Germans were acutely aware of the fact that the Royal Navy still retained a potent force in the eastern Mediterranean. The Germans, even with Italian naval support, lacked the necessary protection for these vulnerable convoys. As the Germans would discover, the Royal Navy was able and willing to interdict and would wreak havoc amongst the German reinforcements.

The German trucks are approaching their final destination. Note the countryside, which is very similar to the terrain that the Germans would encounter on Crete. The roads are poor and follow the hill lines. The area is dotted with olive groves, dry water courses and scrubland. As the Germans would also discover, the communication infrastructure on the island was even worse than that on the mainland.

This appears to be Plieschen astride a donkey in Greece. This hardy creature would prove to be invaluable for both the Germans and the Allies during the battle for Crete. Motor transport was in short supply and in any case the roads were so poor in places that only donkeys could bring up ammunition and food to the most inaccessible positions.

Two Romanian gypsy peddlers are seen here posing with the men on the journey down to Athens.

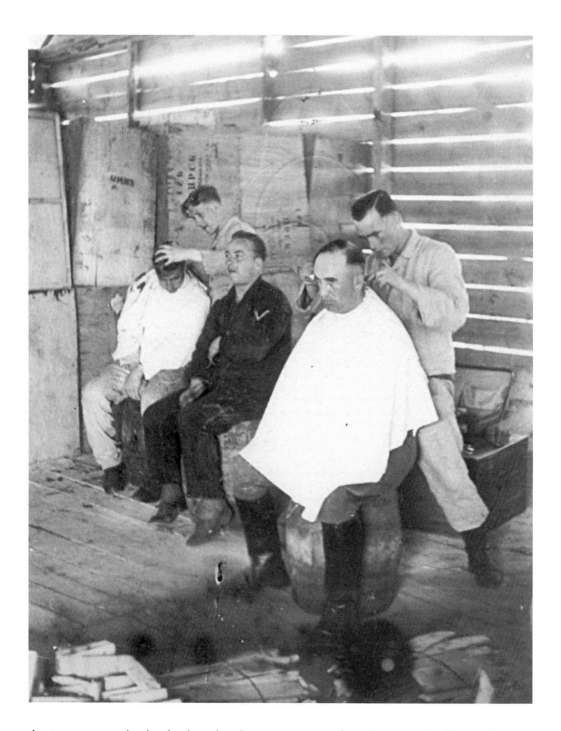

An impromptu barber's shop has been set up in this photograph. The soldier in the centre is a private. None of the men appear to be wearing their jump boots and they have on their fatigue uniforms. This photograph may well have been taken hours before the assault on Crete was launched.

These civilian refugees are probably gypsies. Greek gypsies are also known as *tsiganes* and are considered to be a distinct ethnic minority; for centuries they were nomadic. Ultimately, many of them would share the same fate as the Jewish population of Greece.

This appears to be a Greek public baths or wash house. Here the *Fallschirmjäger* are either washing their own clothes or paying local Greek women to do it for them. Note that even though the men are now on the Greek mainland they can only be identified as *Luftwaffe* personnel and not as *Fallschirmjäger*.

This is a Romany gypsy family. It is not clear exactly how many Romany gypsies were living in Greece in 1941, but like the Jews of Greece they were soon to find themselves in a perilous situation. Many of those in the German-controlled zones were deported. The Bulgarians were equally as fastidious, however the Italians showed little interest and it was not until after 1943, when the Germans took over the Italian occupation areas, that gypsies and Jews in these parts of Greece fell victim to the deportations and exterminations.

The *Fallschirmjäger* are standing amongst the remains of the Acropolis, in the centre of Athens. When the Germans had entered Athens on 27 April 1941 one of the soldiers guarding the Greek flag flying over the Acropolis was told to remove it. He obeyed, wrapped the flag around himself and then threw himself from the walls of the fortress to his death, rather than let the flag fall into enemy hands. This was just the first act of defiance in Athens. Over a month later two eighteen-year-olds, Manolis Glezos and Apostolis Santas, tore down the German flag that was flying over the Acropolis.

This is Syntagma Square in Athens. The ornate building on the right is the Greek parliament. On the skyline to the left is the statue of Athena, over the Hellenic Academy. In the first winter of occupation around 100,000 Greeks died of starvation. Cities such as Athens were particularly badly hit. The bulk of the food was collected and sent to German and Italian troops in North Africa. In Athens people died at such a rate that traditional Orthodox burials were abandoned.

Piraeus harbour, which had been one of the principal ports in which the remnants of the Greek army and the British and Commonwealth troops had used as an evacuation port. Piraeus had been heavily bombed and on 6 April 1941 a munitions ship had been hit. The Germans used Piraeus as one of their major embarkation ports. The convoy carrying the lead elements of the 5th Mountain Division left the harbour on 19 May 1941 and from there it sailed to the island of Milos, arriving there the following day. The convoy left Milos the same evening, just as a second convoy left Piraeus. The first convoy was located by the Royal Navy and despite the presence of an Italian destroyer the bulk of the convoy was destroyed. In effect, the 3rd Battalion of the 100th Mountain Regiment ceased to exist.

Another shot of the Acropolis in Athens, taken in May 1941. Over the centuries the Acropolis has been the victim of several disasters. The most catastrophic was during the Ottoman occupation of Greece. The Parthenon itself was used as a Turkish garrison headquarters and ammunition dump. It suffered enormous damage during the siege of Athens by the Venetians in 1687.

The column makes one final rest stop before arriving for the embarkation ports and airfields in the south of the Greek mainland. Soon the men would be told about the operation and the following is the official brief given to the men regarding the island of Crete:

The island of Crete is approximately 240 km [160 miles] long and varies in width from 12 to 50 km [8 to 35 miles]. The interior is barren and covered by eroded mountains which, in the western part, rise to an elevation of 2,456 m [8,100 ft]. There are few roads and water is scarce. The south coast descends abruptly towards the sea; the only usable port along this part of the coast is the small harbour of Sthion [Hora Sfakion]. There are hardly any north south communications and the only road to Sfhakia [Sfakia] which can be used for motor transportation ends abruptly 1,100 m [3600 ft] above the town. The sole major traffic artery runs close to the north coast and connects Souda Bay with the towns of Maleme, Hania [Chania], Rethymno and Iraklio [Heraklion]. Possession of the north coast is vital for an invader approaching from Greece, if only because of terrain conditions. The British, whose supply bases were situated in Egypt, were greatly handicapped by the fact that the only efficient port is in Souda Bay. The topography of the island, therefore, favoured the invader, particularly since the mountainous terrain left no other alternative to the British but to construct their airfields close to the exposed north coast.

A last chance for a little rest and relaxation before the orders are received for the men to prepare themselves for immediate airlift to Crete. Plieschen's machine gun company would parachute into the area around Rethymno on 20 May 1941. His company would be part of the first and only wave in that region.

Chapter 2

Operation *Mercury*

On 25 October 1940 the German General Franz Halder suggested: 'Mastery of the Eastern Mediterranean was dependent on the capture of Crete, and that this could best be achieved by an air landing.'

Three days later, in a meeting with the Italian dictator Benito Mussolini, Adolf Hitler had told Mussolini that he could make available a whole division of airborne troops and another division of paratroopers should the need arise to take Crete.

The commander of the German XI Air Corps, General Kurt Student, was desperate to prove the value of his new parachute troops in a large and ambitious operation. He had a visionary strategy for the eastern Mediterranean; his men would land and seize Crete. They would then take Cyprus. The ultimate goal would be a paratrooper assault landing on the Suez Canal, to coincide with a major ground offensive launched by Rommel in North Africa. As far as Student was concerned, Crete offered enormous opportunities; it would be difficult for the Allies to launch an effective counter-attack if key points along the north coast were seized.

Ultimately, Hitler was convinced and in the Führer Directive Number 28, dated 25 April 1941, wrote:

> The occupation of the island of Crete (Operation *Merkur*) is to be prepared in order to have a base for conducting the air war against England in the eastern Mediterranean. The transport movements must not lead to any delay in the strategic concentration for *Barbarossa* [the German invasion of Russia].

We have seen how the paratroopers left their bases in Germany and Austria and made their way through Hungary, Romania, Bulgaria and down to the Aegean coast. For many of them the trip seemed rather like a holiday and only when they reached Greece could they see any sign of conflict. Along the roadsides were burned-out vehicles and freshly dug graves. The troops began to concentrate at airfields at Dadion, Eleusis, Megara, Corinth, Tanagra and Topolia.

On 15 May regimental and battalion commanders met with Student at the Hotel Grande Bretagne on Syntagma Square in Athens. Technically this was a *Luftwaffe* operation. Close support for the landings came in the shape of the VIII Air Corps, which had around 570 aircraft. Transport planes were being concentrated at the airfields, the most important of which were over 500 Junkers 52s. Operation *Merkur* (Mercury) was originally scheduled for 17 May, but due to the delay in receiving 5,000 tons of aviation fuel it was pushed back to 20 May.

Student outlined the key elements of the operation. His storm regiment of four battalions would land around the airfield at Maleme on the west of the island. The 3rd Regiment would drop near Hania. Our man Plieschen would be part of the drop that would land 50 km further east, along with the 2nd Regiment, with the job of seizing the airfield near Rethymno. The 1st Regiment was tasked with seizing the airfield at Heraklion 65 km further east. Troops in gliders would land first then paratroopers. Once the airfields had been taken the 5th Mountain Division and other units would be brought in by transport aircraft. Simultaneously, probably on day two of the operation, upwards of seventy small vessels would bring in additional reinforcements and anti-aircraft units. There would also be an opportunity to reinforce with tanks and motor transport.

The Germans had estimated that the garrison on Crete was no more than 5,000 strong. The Germans expected no opposition at Rethymno and believed that Heraklion was only lightly held. They also believed that the bulk of the Commonwealth forces had not in fact been evacuated from the Greek mainland to Crete, but straight to Egypt. Additionally, the Germans believed there were no Greek troops on the island. To their horror they would discover that they were wrong on every single count.

Whilst the Germans' intelligence reports were at best misleading, the commander of Allied troops on Crete had a far better picture of the Germans' intentions. Major General Bernard Freyberg VC had reached Crete on 29 April 1941. He fully expected to only be there for a matter of days and that ultimately his task would be to reassemble all of the New Zealand troops in Egypt. His whistle-stop inspection of the island's defences and available troops left him with a heavy heart and this was compounded when it was confirmed that he would command Creforce. Freyberg was in fact the seventh commander on the island since November 1940. He had one major advantage; he was privy to the cracked intercepts that had been made in German military signals. As the days toward the launching of Operation *Mercury* passed it became more and more clear what the Germans were intending.

The Germans had one major advantage – total and undisputed air superiority. Mercilessly they bombarded known British positions on the island and each time there was an expectation that the air attacks were just a prelude to a major parachute landing. Nothing, however, occurred until 20 May. What the Germans did not know was that instead of 5,000, or even a pessimistic 11,000, there were in fact 48,000 British, Commonwealth and Allied troops on Crete. Admittedly, many of the men were in depleted battalions; others lacked transport and even weapons, but the Germans were about to drop into a cauldron of destruction and death. The balance of the island's fate would hang on such a threadbare line that it could snap at any time.

A Ju52 takes off from an airfield on mainland Greece, bound for Crete. The commander of the 1,500 troops earmarked to land around Rethymno, Colonel Alfred Sturm, had already distinguished himself at the head of his 2nd Parachute Regiment. It had been his men that had captured the Corinth Canal. Delays seemed to follow delays and the departure of aircraft heading for Maleme and for the Ayia Valley pushed back his schedule. As the Ju52s returned for refuelling and to pick up Sturm's men, it became abundantly clear to them that there would be a hot reception awaiting them. Many of the Ju52s were bullet ridden; some needed to be patched up before they were fully airworthy.

Each of the three motors on the Ju52s had to be refuelled by hand as there were no petrol bowsers. Eager to get going, the paratroopers helped out, stripping off all their combat gear and working in gym clothes in the almost unbearable 40°C heat. Everywhere there was swirling red dust and all attempts to water the runways failed as the water quickly evaporated in the heat. Even as the men began to pack their gear they found the aircraft stiflingly hot.

Sturm's men had been due to be dropping on Rethymno by 1400 hours, but as we see in this picture the men were still sitting around and waiting and had not even got into the aircraft. Finally, the first wave of aircraft got underway, creating even more dust and holding up subsequent waves. The delays would prove to be crucial, as each pause between a wave gave the defenders times to recover. Sturm knew that he had a tough task ahead of him; he had had to reluctantly hand over his 2nd Battalion to Colonel Bruno Bräuer's 1st Parachute Regiment to reinforce his attack on Heraklion airport.

Sturm retained a reinforced company under his own command and then divided the rest of the regiment into two groups; the first being led by Major Kroh who would land to the east of the airfield. The other group, led by Captain Wiedemann, would land closest to Rethymno itself. Sturm would land in the centre. Attached to each of the groups was a machine gun unit and it is not clear precisely to which company Plieschen was attached. The men only expected weak resistance. It was Sturm's opinion that he should be able to link his men quickly and then detach a force to move west to link up with more airborne troops that had landed around Souda Bay, near Hania.

The men of Plieschen's unit on board a Ju52, bound for Crete. Each of the Ju52s was capable of carrying around twelve men plus their equipment. The men would land only armed with their pistol and grenades. Some may have had machine guns slung around their necks. For the precious seconds that they were dropping from the air they would be incredibly vulnerable to attack from the ground. Of Sturm's force Major Kroh would have around 550 men reinforced by a machine gun company. His orders were to land to the east of the airfield and capture it. Some 800 men, again with a machine gun company under Wiedemann, were tasked with seizing Rethymno itself. Sturm's force was around 200 strong.

Facing them below was Lieutenant Colonel Ian Campbell who had two Australian battalions, each with around 600 men. He could also call on ninety Australian gunners, two platoons of machine gunners, 800 Cretan police and 2,300 Greek infantry. The latter often lacked rifles and those that did have firearms had barely ten rounds each. The supply situation for the other units was equally as poor; there were only around five rounds for each anti-tank rifle and the four available 3-in mortars had just eighty bombs. The medium machine guns had around sixteen belts of ammunition per weapon. Very few of the men had reserves of rifle ammunition and there were very few grenades. The men's uniforms were in a deplorable state and their boots were full of holes.

A stunning view out of the window of a Ju52, as the aircraft flies along the Cretan coast towards their drop zones. The outcome of the battle around Rethymno depended on who controlled the low foothills. The airfield itself was to the south of the road. It was five miles from Rethymno and about 500 metres from the beach. Around the east of the airfield was a steep plateau, which Campbell had named Hill A. There were two gullies to the west and beyond that a ridge, labelled Hill D. After a second gully was Hill B and finally, about a mile from Rethymno itself, was Hill C. It would be these areas that would see the bulk of the fighting.

There is a clear sense of apprehension on the faces of these German paratroopers as they make their last preparations as the aircraft comes in towards Rethymno. Below, Campbell's main priority was the defence of the airfield. He spread his men along the foothills, with the idea that he would be able to sweep the coastal plain with fire whilst his men remained relatively safe in cover. Campbell's two Australian battalions occupied Hills A and B, with the 4th Greek battalion sandwiched in between. Campbell's force reserve was the 5th Greek Battalion, in a valley that separated the coastal ridge from the hills. He had a pair of Matilda tanks, which would be used for a counter-attack if the Germans tried to seize the airstrip. Parts of Hills A and B had barbed wire and where possible the men had strengthened their defensive positions. Campbell had a ragtag of artillery, mainly old French and Italian field guns. There were no anti-aircraft guns.

The door of the Ju52 is open and we can see two other aircraft in the same flight, flying in formation. In the far distance we can see the Cretan coastline. This photograph must have been taken literally a few minutes before the aircraft began their approach on the drop zone. The Germans had tried to carry out photoreconnaissance over Rethymno. A reconnaissance aircraft had been shot down and from it the British had found a photograph, dated 8 May. On it was marked a company position. Campbell abandoned this position and redeployed the unit. The Germans had launched their last reconnaissance flight on 18 May and still believed that the paratroopers would come up against very little opposition on the ground. In all probability Sturm's men had been selected for what they believed to be the easiest of the operations, as a result of the casualties that he had suffered when they had landed to seize the Corinth Canal.

Below, at 0900 hours on 20 May, Campbell's men had watched flights of Ju52s heading towards Hania. The Rethymno area had come under air attack at 1600 hours. Twenty or so German fighters and light bombers had searched the plain and the hills for targets. Some of the Greek recruits had panicked, but Australians were sent to get them back into position. Suddenly, at around 1615 hours, an enormous number of Ju52s, which Campbell knew to be troop carriers, appeared over the sea. They made for the coast near Heraklion, some splitting off but others continuing west along the coast.

Another view out of the window of the Ju52, with a second aircraft clearly visible but slightly lower, below the left wing. Campbell's men could see around 160 Ju52s passing close to the hillsides. The defenders opened up with everything they had and seven of the aircraft were brought down, crash-landing along the beach. Some others were also hit and limped back out to sea on fire. In one of the units the platoon commander was shot dead in the doorway as he prepared to jump and his men were so panicked that they refused to jump. On this aircraft the pilot circled round, but as he came in a second time one of the engines was hit and it caught fire. The pilot managed to crash-land into the sea and the paratroopers clambered out and got into a dinghy; of the men that escaped the aircraft only two would be alive at the end of the day. By the time the Ju52s began dropping men around the Rethymno area it was about 1700 hours.

This is another view from the window of the Ju52. A member of the headquarters company of the 2nd *Fallschirmjäger* regiment, Rudolf Adler, described the scene as the aircraft approached the drop zone:

> We spotted the island and the aircraft went down. AA fire started. Events rushed by. Bullets were ripping through the body of the aircraft at head height. The first three jumpers fell on the floor of the aircraft. We approached the door; it was blocked by the bodies of the dead and our bundles. Everybody was shouting 'Out! Out!' The engine started coughing; there was black smoke. Impossible to think but the instinct for survival was there. I don't remember how I left the aircraft.

This view is from a different window of the Ju52; this time it is clear that the aircraft is considerably lower than before. Dropping onto a position such as the one chosen for this operation was fraught with difficulties. If the paratroopers were dropped too early there was a likelihood that they would fall into the sea and be drowned by the weight of their equipment and the silk canopies. If they were dropped too far inland the danger was that they would land on rocky terrain and either injure or kill themselves as they hit the ground. In fact, there was an even worse fate for twelve men – a whole Ju52's worth of paratroopers. They landed on top of a bamboo cane windbreak between fields and were impaled on the canes. The first drop would consist of 1,380 *Fallschirmjäger*; most of them were dropped in the wrong place. Adler explained:

> Because of the enemy fire, the *Fallschirmjäger* left their aircraft earlier than planned and missed their drop zone, the weapon containers dropped into enemy-held territory and we jumped directly over their lines. Hours later I found the first three of my surviving comrades.

The low hills along the Cretan coast can be clearly seen in this photograph. Behind them are the higher and rockier hills and beyond them the beginning of the mountain range, which extends from west to east almost as far as Rethymno. This photograph probably shows the mountain range that lies between Rethymno and Heraklion. This is the second of the three mountain ranges on the island. So indiscriminate were the parachute drops that only two of the companies in the entire operation were dropped in the right place. Major Kroh, the commander of the 3rd Battalion, along with a complete company, was dropped three miles to the east of the airfield that had been his objective. To add to the insult there was also injury, as the men fell on ground so rocky that a number of them broke bones. The two companies that did land on target, on the airfield, landed slap bang in front of Campbell's positions. As soon as the Germans that had landed here knew the peril that they now faced some wanted to surrender. One of the sergeants took control and led them out of the impossible position to join up with Kroh's main force.

This is a perplexing photograph, as it does not appear to have been taken from the Ju52 and may well be out of sequence in the photo album. It shows a flight of German aircraft, almost certainly Ju52s. If indeed this photograph was taken once Plieschen had landed this must have been just minutes after he dropped onto Cretan soil. Most of Kroh's men fell around the olive oil factory at Stavromenos, some two kilometres away from the airfield. As quickly as he could he tried to regroup his force and make for Hill A. Kroh's group had landed to the far east of the drop zone. Between them and the landing strip was an entire Australian battalion.

A last shot of the *Fallschirmjäger*, as they prepare to parachute out of the aircraft. Sergeant Plieschen referred to having fallen and fought around what he called Vineyard Hill, or Bloody Hill, so this may help us to identify precisely where he was engaged during the operation. This indicates that he almost certainly landed with Kroh's group, as Hill A was known as Bloody Hill by those involved in the engagement. The maelstrom into which the paratroopers would jump would be a nightmare. The paratroopers did not have tropical uniforms and were heavily laden with all of their equipment. As the aircraft made their way along the coast of Crete they should have been escorted by fighter aircraft, but the paratroopers could see through the windows that the fighters were actually heading back for refuelling; everything was out of sync.

This is the rugged coastline of Crete, as seen from the window of the Ju52. Despite the fact that Crete lies relatively close to the North African coast of Libya, its countryside is quite lush and is covered in olive trees. The aircraft came in around 1600 hours and the men were told that they would be dropping at a height of around 500 feet. As the aircraft reached the drop zone they came under anti-aircraft and field gun fire. Aircraft were dropping out of the sky. Desperately, the pilots nursed their machines on course to give the paratroopers the chance to jump out. Many of the aircraft would not make it back home.

This is a second view of the peninsula on the coast of Crete. It is likely that this shot was taken literally minutes before the aircraft reached the drop zone, as the Ju52 is skirting the coastline, hunting for the drop zone. Below, the Australians could hear the hum as the aircraft approached. The Ju52s were preceded by Dorniers, which dropped smoke flares to indicate the landing areas. Australian eye witnesses reported seeing eight or nine groups of around eighteen Ju52 troop-carrying aircraft. They came in three or four minutes apart and turned west at the coast around a mile from the drop zone. Plieschen was one of those that dropped in the area between the olive oil factory at Stavromenos, over the airstrip and as far as the village of Perivolia. Around 1,600 men dropped and one of the eye witnesses was in an observation slip trench on the east side of Hill A. He had a telephone linked to brigade headquarters. After reporting the incoming flights and the number of aircraft, he shook hands with his signaller and said, 'We may have five or six minutes to live but we will get a few before we die.'

The last moment of calm and contemplation for the paratroopers, who are now ready for their jump into the unknown. The main part of Kroh's battle group, of which Plieschen and his fellow paratroopers were a part, had aimed to be dropped directly on the airfield, but the main part fell around the olive oil factory two kilometres to the east. Very quickly the paratroopers would not only realise that they had dropped into a killing zone, but also that German intelligence, which had led them to believe that the airfield was unprotected, was far from correct.

This is a fascinating photograph, which was presumably taken moments after Plieschen had landed on Cretan soil. We can see a flight of three Ju52 aircraft about to pass overhead. In the distance three or four minutes behind them is another flight. The beach is to the rear of the photograph and off to the left, indicating that this is a shot taken to the east and that Hill A is actually behind Plieschen. Note that the terrain consists of scrubland but in the foreground there is a wheat field. It is likely that this is the outskirts of Stavromenos, as scattered buildings can be seen in the centre of the photograph. Stavromenos would prove to be an important position in this part of the struggle for the island of Crete. The paratroopers had been dispersed and in fact the paratrooper group of which Plieschen was a part had been dropped over a five-mile area. Very soon after this photograph was taken Kroh was desperately trying to organise his men for an assault on Hill A.

This photograph amply illustrates just how dispersed the parachute drops were around Rethymno. Here we can see dozens of German paratroopers, along with their weapons canisters, floating down towards the Cretan countryside. This photograph looks to the west. Hill A is just in view on the extreme left. Plieschen has now taken cover in the wheat field. Far in the distance we can see Rethymno, which sits on a promontory. These men may well have been those that dropped on and around Hill A, literally amongst the Australians. Campbell, in his command post on Hill D, could see that his own men and the German paratroopers were intermingled. Lieutenant Dieppe was with the Australians on Hill A and described his first encounter with the enemy:

I saw one of our 2/1 MG battalion machine guns being enveloped by a parachute. At the same time one parachutist landed almost on top of me, and immediately surrendered. He was shaking like a leaf. I saw a parachutist throwing a stick grenade whilst still in the air.

Another photograph, this one taken seconds later, of the parachute drop. We can see that some of the paratroopers have landed close to the coast, whilst others have drifted toward Hill A. Other paratroopers are still descending from the skies. The Australian official history of the event describes it as:

> ...a bitter series of fights between sections or platoons of Australians on the one hand and, on the other, such groups of paratroops who survived long enough to organise and go into action.

It is important to bear in mind that the paratroopers were often landing just with grenades or a pistol, although others had slung machine pistols around their necks. Most of the weapons were still in the containers, which they needed to retrieve before they were fully operational.

These German paratroopers were dropping around Stavromenos and the olive oil factory. Kroh had headed west with his company, collecting up the survivors of 2 Company MG Battalion 7, of which Plieschen was a member. He gathered together elements of the 10th and 12th Companies of the 3rd Battalion; by mistake they, too, had been dropped to the east of the airfield.

A photograph showing more paratroopers landing further east, possibly around the airfield, or these may be men of Wiedemann's group, which landed closer to Perivolia. This photograph certainly dispels the myth that Crete was a barren wasteland; we can see a number of olive trees in the foreground, which would have been a major hazard to the paratroopers. However, they were to come to love these trees, as they would provide them with vital cover in the hours to come. Far to the west, around Rethymno, some 800 Cretan *gendarmes*, led by Major Christos Tsiphakis, a Cretan officer, lay in wait for the Germans. As soon as the German paratroopers started landing Campbell realised that he would have to commit his reserves as soon as possible. He did not lack decisiveness, but elsewhere the men on the ground were perfectly capable of taking the initiative against the invaders. As Kroh made his way towards Hill A he came across Lieutenant von Roon. The lieutenant had gathered some men together and was hotly engaged by Cretan irregulars. As Kroh and his force arrived they managed to overcome the defenders and they killed the field gun and machine gun crews. They were then able to use the vineyards as cover.

This is an excellent photograph of a German paratrooper stealthily moving towards Stavromenos, in the hope that he would find more of his unit. This man has obviously retrieved his rifle from a weapons' canister. Overhead we can see at least three more flights of Ju52s coming into the drop zones. Pretty soon the attack on Hill A would be developing. As the official Australian historian recounted:

> On the east of the line paratroopers landed on top of one platoon of infantry, the 75-mm guns, and the two Vickers guns, under Lieutenant Cleaver. Crew after crew of the Vickers guns were shot down, and the guns were finally put out of action by a German mortar bomb. The surviving gunners of the 75s, who had no small arms except three pistols, withdrew to the battery head-quarters further up the ridge, carrying their breech blocks with them.

Such was the determination of the defenders that this gun crew fought on well into the night. They held their position and fired at the advancing paratroopers with captured German weapons.

This is one of the last photographs of the landings. Things did not go well for the Germans. Colonel Sturm's group, comprising nearly 200 men, had dropped right in front of an Australian battalion. Sturm and his headquarters staff were lucky enough to drop into dead ground. Casualties were enormous and before night-fall around eighty-eight prisoners had been taken and Sturm himself was captured the following morning. Kroh's determined attack on Hill A had succeeded in over-whelming the Australian positions.

Campbell now determined to stop them from advancing east from Hill A and onto the airfield. His two Matilda tanks of the 7th Royal Tank Regiment, under Lieutenant George Simpson, met an early disaster; one fell into a drainage ditch and Simpson was killed and the second one slid into a gulley 10 feet deep and could provide no further support. Campbell regrouped his infantry and tried to retake Hill A but the paratroopers now had excellent cover in the terraces. At 0525 hours on 21 May 1941 the Australians launched a counter-attack against Hill A; it quickly ground to a halt but some of the Australians had managed to get a toe hold on the south-west corner of the hill. Campbell collected up every man, cooks, gunners and signallers included, and at 0800 hours another counter-attack was made on Hill A. This time they took a number of prisoners and the Germans fell back. In fact, the number of prisoners taken was beginning to become a problem. Ultimately, Kroh had to fall back to the olive oil factory and beat off repeated attacks.

This photograph was taken in Rethymno after the fighting had been concluded. By dawn on 22 May Campbell was ready to launch an attack on the olive oil factory. He began the assault by firing what remained of his artillery and then it was planned for an assault to be made at dawn. As it was, the attack went in at 1000 hours but it was beaten off by rifle fire. Another attack was prepared for 1800 hours but once again this failed and the Australians fell back to Hill A, leaving Greek troops to surround the factory. There was a short truce on 23 May and a *Fallschirmjäger* officer appeared with a white flag, but instead of offering his surrender he invited Campbell to surrender; the offer was declined. It would not be until the morning of 26 May that Campbell's eastern flank would be secured and the olive oil factory captured, but by then many of the *Fallschirmjäger* had slipped east.

German troops are looking over a captured Bren gun carrier in this photograph. Allied transport on Crete was fairly limited, as much of it had been abandoned during the evacuation of mainland Greece. The events that had taken place at Rethymno were overshadowed by German reinforcement of their landings at Maleme and in the Prison Valley area near Chania. The Germans' attack on Heraklion had similarly met with stiff resistance and heavy casualties. In the Rethymno area, once Maleme had fallen and the Germans were able to pour in additional troops, including mountain units, onto the island, the battle was clearly lost. A large number of German motorcyclists had entered Rethymno on the evening of 29 May 1941; German tanks had also been landed. Still the island's defenders put up a stiff fight, denying the Germans each inch. Reluctantly, Colonel Campbell, still on Hill D, ordered a white flag to be made as the Germans closed. He realised that any further fighting would be a senseless loss of life. They turned in 500 German prisoners, including Sturm. The Australians had lost around 120 killed and they had managed to kill more than 500 German paratroopers.

A second shot of the Germans looking over a Bren gun carrier. The evacuation of Allied troops from Crete began on the night of 29 May and continued through until I June. Several whole battalions, or at least what remained of them, had to be left behind, although some battalions were more fortunate and half escaped to fight again from Egypt. The roads heading towards the south coast were strewn with abandoned equipment and vehicles. There was simply no time for the men to even contemplate trying to repair broken down vehicles, or to find fuel. The retreating columns were under constant air attack.

German troops settle into billets in Rethymno. The last Allied ships left the Cretan coast before dawn on I June. The Allies were forced to leave 9,000 men behind. Most of the infantry had come down to the coast on foot and many of them had turned to act as a rearguard, holding back the Germans for as long as possible. It had been an exhausting campaign, albeit a brief one. The retreating Allies had been pursued by mountain troops, as one *Gerbirgsjäger* recalled:

> Every group has its wounded and yet we carry on with unheard of élan. We no longer feel the heat and have overcome extreme exhaustion. Below us is the sea and port of Safakion with the white cubes of its serried buildings. The rugged mountains drop steeply to the ground below.

A street scene in Rethymno; note the mix of vehicles parked along the street, including a captured Bren gun carrier, which has been pressed into action by the Germans. The Allies destroyed as much equipment as possible as they retreated. Even though many of the units towards the end were unarmed, exhausted and hungry they had still been machine-gunned by *Luftwaffe* aircraft. The formal surrender took place at the foot of the Imbros Gorge, when Lieutenant Colonel Theo Walker, an Australian battalion commander, found himself the senior officer left on the island. Walker followed the track up to the village of Komitades and here he found an Austrian officer of the 100th Mountain Regiment. The Austrian spoke first:

'What are you doing here, Australia?'

Walker replied, 'One might ask what are you doing here, Austria?'

'We are all Germans,' replied the Austrian.

This is a shot of one of the many requisitioned Greek civilian sailing vessels that were used by the Germans to ferry in reinforcements during the invasion of Crete. These relatively flimsy wooden vessels proved to be death traps for many of the German reinforcements when they were intercepted by Royal Naval vessels. On 22 May 1941 Admiral Cunningham, based in Alexandria, had despatched Rear Admiral King's Force C to intercept flotillas of German vessels. The three cruisers and four destroyers made short work of many of the German-held vessels and the German air cover did not dare risk bombing Royal Navy vessels for fear of hitting their own ships.

This is a view of the Venetian harbour and Turkish lighthouse at Rethymno. The mole was built in around 1300 and the lighthouse in the seventeenth century. For centuries the harbour was used to build and moor Venetian galleys and Turkish warships. The masts of some of the vessels that were used by the Germans can be seen behind the buildings, on the left hand side of the photograph. By the evening of 29 May 1941 the Australian troops that remained in the Rethymno area were virtually cut off. A Greek officer had arrived and told Campbell that the British had left Heraklion and that not only was Rethymno now menaced from the west, but also from the east. All through that night Australian soldiers had tried to use signals to attract Royal Navy warships, hoping that an evacuation might be mounted. The Germans renewed their advance on the port the following day and it was clear that Rethymno was doomed.

What appears to be a German headquarters and billet near the seafront at Rethymno. For the paratroopers, even after the surrender, their job was not yet over. For some time they would be involved in rounding up Allied stragglers, guarding the prisoners and trying to secure the island. Amongst those captured were Spanish republicans, who feared that the Germans would turn them over to Franco, when they would be shot. The battalion medical officer, Captain Cochrane, who had served with the international brigades in Spain, suggested that the men pretend that they were Gibraltarians. Not all of the men that missed the evacuation transport were captured. Some would be taken off by submarine, others would live in the mountains, and some would try to escape in tiny boats across the Libyan Sea. Years later the skeleton of a soldier was discovered high up in the mountains; he had clearly fallen from the cliff and had laid there undisturbed.

A German soldier rides a mule. Many of these beasts were brought over to the island by the Germans themselves, primarily by the mountain troops. Additional waves of German reinforcements had spread out across the island. The Germans ran into what appeared to be enemy light tanks beyond Aghios Nikolaos, to the far east of the island. They were about to engage and a German officer went forward to investigate. He found the tanks belonged to the Italians, who had landed at Sitia unopposed on 28 May.

This is an unidentified merchant ship on fire and close to sinking off the Cretan coast. Note that this is an armed vessel, as it has at least one deck-mounted gun. The seas around Crete had seen the loss of several Royal Navy vessels, in addition to the ships that the Germans had lost during the invasion. Amongst these was HMS *Greyhound*, a G-class British destroyer sunk by Stukas on 22 May 1941, and the light cruiser HMS *Fiji*, which was straddled by twenty bombs. Many of the crew were rescued by HMS *Kandahar* and HMS *Kingston*.

The streets of Rethymno are strewn with rubble, showing signs of the intense fighting in and around the port. Colonel Campbell had refused to retreat from Rethymno until he had received explicit orders to do so. In some respects the Allies were very lucky, as they streamed south towards the coast and the evacuation ports. A large number of the fighters and bombers had already been recalled for the impending invasion of Russia plus Campbell's troops were only pursued by a single regiment.

Lew Lind was a nineteen-year-old soldier in the Australian 2/3 Field Regiment. They had fought hard to hold the Germans off at Rethymno and on the night of 29 May they were still in position around the airfield. On the morning of 31 May, German tanks and motorcycle troops arrived. Lind and a few others tried to run for it, but two of them were shot. They were captured and marched west without food and sent on to Chania before going on to Maleme. They were forced to march for sixty miles with little food and water in the blazing sun. Lind and the others were forced to clear the airfield. By 12 June only about half of the men were left; the others had succumbed to dysentery.

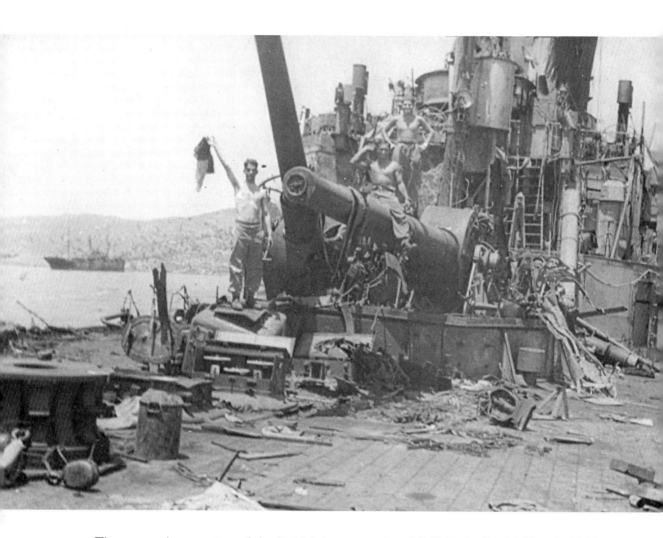

These are the remains of the British heavy cruiser HMS *York*. On 26 March 1941 she had been attacked by the Italians. The previous night the Italian destroyers *Crispi* and *Sella* had managed to get close to Souda Bay and they launched six one-man high-speed explosive motorboats. The vessels were so tiny that they got over the anti-submarine nets and boom and made for their target. One of the motorboats hit HMS *York*; she was the largest warship in Souda Bay. She was extremely badly damaged. The Royal Navy was forced to ground her in an attempt to save her from sinking, but a few days later she was devastated by a German air attack. HMS *York* was wrecked by the Royal Navy using demolition charges on 22 May 1941 and by this time some of her guns had been taken away and used as land-based artillery.

This is a second shot of HMS *York*. Attempts had been made to try to save her and the British submarine HMS *Rover* had been sent from Alexandria, but the submarine had been attacked by German aircraft and the salvage attempt had been abandoned. HMS *York* had been launched in 1928 and completed on 6 May 1930. She had been the eleventh Royal Navy ship to carry the name and had already seen service in the Atlantic in 1939 and off Norway in 1940. In August 1940 she had been transferred to the Mediterranean Fleet and in October had been in Malta. After sailing to Alexandria in late 1940 she had reached Crete in January 1941 and was engaged in covering the military convoys to Greece. HMS *York* was salvaged in 1952 and was towed into Bari in Italy to be broken up in the March.

This photograph is believed to portray Major Erich Schulz, who was commander of the machine gun company between June 1940 and August 1941. He is clearly a major from the design of his epaulettes. We can clearly see his *Fallschirmjäger* collar tabs, his parachuter's badge pinned to the bottom right and he also wears an officer's peaked cap, probably in tropical tan. The parachute regiment had its own distinctive cap badge. There was another Major Schulz on Crete at the same time; he was in command of the 1st Battalion of the 1st Regiment of *Fallschirmjäger* and his men dropped around Heraklion. We can also see his *Luftwaffe* officer's cap reef and the *Luftwaffe* eagle that was worn on the breast.

Schulz is awarding medals of gallantry to the members of the machine gun company in this picture. Note that the men are now in tropical dress, with shorts. Some are wearing jack boots whilst others are wearing their jump boots. The two men on the right of the photograph are *obergefreiters*. They have simple shoulder straps and one of them has the three eagles on his collar. All of the men retain their sidearms. Schulz appears to be decorating the men with the Iron Cross, dispensed from a mess tin.

In order to win the Iron Cross a soldier would have to display three to five acts of bravery above and beyond the call of duty. Soldiers would initially be awarded with the Iron Cross Second Class for one act of bravery. This would then be one of the requirements to win the Iron Cross First Class. During the war the Germans awarded some three million Iron Cross Second Class decorations and 450,000 Iron Cross First Class. As for the men in this photograph, it is difficult to know precisely whether they were amongst the 500 German prisoners that had been scooped up by Campbell's forces by 25 May 1941. They were all held on the southern side of Hill D.

The handing out of the awards has now been completed. Note that it appears that only the men to the extreme left have been presented with gallantry awards. The man closest to Schulz, on the extreme right of the photograph, is a *gefreiter*. The paratrooper carrying the mess tin, standing next to Schulz, seems to be either a *feldwebel* or an *oberfeldwebel*, although it is difficult to see from the angle of the photograph. Due to the similarity between the M1936, M1937 (two variants) and the M1938 model paratroopers' helmets it is difficult to be sure which variation the men are wearing. In all probability the thickness of the chin straps indicate that these are M1938 versions and would have either been painted in grey or apple green. The shape and style of the eagle on the left hand side of the helmet is typical of either the first or second model eagle, which was standard *Luftwaffe* insignia for these helmets. If indeed these are the M1938 helmets then they would have heavy rubber padding on the sides and the crown. Helmet sizing was achieved by varying the thickness of the rubber padding, but there were four different shell sizes.

Schulz can be seen here with his own Iron Cross above his parachutist's badge. The photograph also indicates that the non-commissioned officer is likely to be a *feldwebel*. Lieutenant-Colonel Ian Campbell, during the height of the fighting around the olive oil factory and at Perivolia, had been faced with having to contend with a number of German prisoners and a large number of wounded. Undoubtedly, the presence of the battalion medical officer, Dr Alan Carter, not only saved the lives of many Commonwealth troops but also the wounded paratroopers:

> As soon as we had recaptured Hill A and the country to its west, Captain Carter and his stretcher bearers had moved east of Hill A down into the flat narrow coastal strip 800 yards across which to the east stood the factory. I agreed Captain Carter should try to arrange a truce with the Germans, so that our own and the paratroop wounded could be cared for. Captain Carter, under a white flag, then walked east to the factory and arranged a three-hour truce.

More of the unit receiving the congratulations on their gallantry from Schulz. Note the differences in the style of helmets worn. The helmet worn by the man shaking hands with Schulz is undoubtedly an M1937 variant, probably in *Luftwaffe* blue with the traditional national colours of Imperial Germany on the side. In this picture we can also see the belt and buckle worn by the man nearest to the camera. The buckle consists of a wreath surrounding a German eagle carrying a swastika.

It is clear that even some of the less injured German paratroopers owed their lives to the prompt work of Captain Carter and two German doctors and their staff, who operated from an isolated two-roomed shack 300 yards to the east of Hill A. The two German doctors had made a gentleman's agreement with Carter to work on all wounded, but as prisoners. Carter remained with the Germans at the aid post until 29 May, when it was closed down.

On the evening of 21 May 1941 a column of wounded, both Commonwealth and German, was being transported to Adhele. The *Luftwaffe* attacked the column and one of the German doctors was killed. The medical staff used both Commonwealth and German drugs and medical equipment, and they shared the same rations equally.

Schulz pins an Iron Cross onto the chest of one of the men in his unit. Colonel Campbell was clearly impressed by the calibre of the German paratroopers:

On the afternoon of 23 May, a force of seventy paratroops (wounded) marched out of the factory to surrender to us, as they could not be cared for by the Germans in the factory, apparently. We [Captain Carter] accepted them and they were sent on from the ex-German aid post by Carter to Adhele. We captured the factory on the morning of 26 May and we found that most of the paratroops had fled during the previous night leaving a small fit guard and about forty more wounded to surrender to us. The paratroops were the finest-looking group of young men I have ever met. Hand-picked. They fought bravely and fairly. We had 500 of them as prisoners of war, so I saw a lot of them. There was no real alternative my troops and I could take in caring for the German wounded. An unsuccessful parachute landing will always end up with the defenders having to care for the wounded paratroops.

This photograph features Plieschen, whose shoulder tabs are somewhat confusing. He is variously described as being a *hauptfeldwebel* (company sergeant major) or a *stabsfeldwebel* (effectively a sergeant). It does appear that he has two pips on his shoulder tab in this picture, which would indicate that he is an *oberfeldwebel*, or platoon leader. Certainly the four wings on his lapel indicate that he is at least this rank, as four were worn by *oberfeldwebels* and *stabsfeldwebels*. A number of men close to him in his unit were killed during the air assault on Crete and it is not precisely clear as to whether or not he was captured during the fighting and subsequently released, or whether he evaded capture.

The congratulations and awards continue in this photograph. Note that in the distance there is an armed *Fallschirmjäger* on guard. Even after the surrender of the Commonwealth forces on the island Crete remained a dangerous place for German soldiers. During the fighting Cretans had used rusty old guns, agricultural tools and even sticks to defend their homes. The Germans had reacted with harshness and brutality, mounting reprisals against the armed resistance movement that grew in strength every day.

The Cretan resistance and civilians assisted the many hundreds of Commonwealth troops that had failed to reach the evacuation beaches in time. The Cretans hid and fed them and guided them down to lonely beaches and coves to be picked up by submarines. The resistance movement was one of the most successful of the war, operating in conjunction with the British Special Operations Executive. Many Greeks would also return to the island to operate in the resistance.

One of the high points was the capture of General Kreipe. In the spring of 1944, the Allies planned to kidnap General Müller, 'the Butcher of Crete'. However, by the time the operation could be launched by the SOE and Cretan resistance, Müller had left the island and had been replaced by General Kreipe. He was snatched on 26 April 1944 and despite being hunted by thousands of German troops, the kidnap party crossed the mountains and reached the south coast where they were picked up a British motor launch on 14 May. Kreipe was taken to Egypt for interrogation, later being imprisoned in Canada and then Wales. He was released in 1947.

Members of the machine gun unit are proudly posing after receiving their Iron Cross decorations. It is interesting to note that two of the men are wearing jack boots whilst the rest wear their *Fallschirmjäger* boots. Also note that some of the men are not wearing regulation belt buckles, notably the two men in the centre, who may well be officers in the unit. So outraged were the German authorities regarding the attacks on the paratroopers by Cretan civilians that Goering ordered Student to make a judicial enquiry and to carry out immediate reprisals. The process took three months and Judge Schölz, in a preliminary report written on 4 June 1941, wrote: 'Many parachutists were subjected to inhumane treatment or mutilated [and] Greek civilians participated in the fight.'

A more balanced study showed that there were only around twenty-five cases on the entire island and most of these were post mortem injuries. At Kondomari sixty civilians were shot, at Kastelli Kissamou 200 Greek men were executed and special action squads roamed across the island indiscriminately slaughtering civilians and destroying villages.

This is another shot of the awards ceremony. Whilst Student's *Fallschirmjäger* and the mountain troops had scored a remarkable victory over the Commonwealth troops on Crete it had been touch and go. They had suffered appalling casualties. As it was, Crete (as a strategic position) never lived up to either the Germans' or the Allies' expectations. Crete was never used as a major base against Allied forces in North Africa and Greece was never chosen as a primary target by the Allies; instead the first Allies to step foot back on the European mainland did so in Italy. Even Hitler concluded: 'The day of the *Fallschirmjäger* is passed.'

Student referred to Crete as: 'The grave of German airborne forces.'

A post-award ceremony celebration is shown in this photograph. The men are wearing a mixture of uniforms; some have the M1941 *Luftwaffe* cotton shirt or are wearing the tropical tunic and matching trousers. Others are more formally dressed, with their *flieger* blouse. Occupied Crete was ultimately divided into a German and an Italian zone. The east was Italian but the Germans occupied three of the provinces, with garrisons in the major towns and smaller outposts scattered throughout the countryside. The southern coast became a prohibited zone, with linked guard posts to try to prevent clandestine landings.

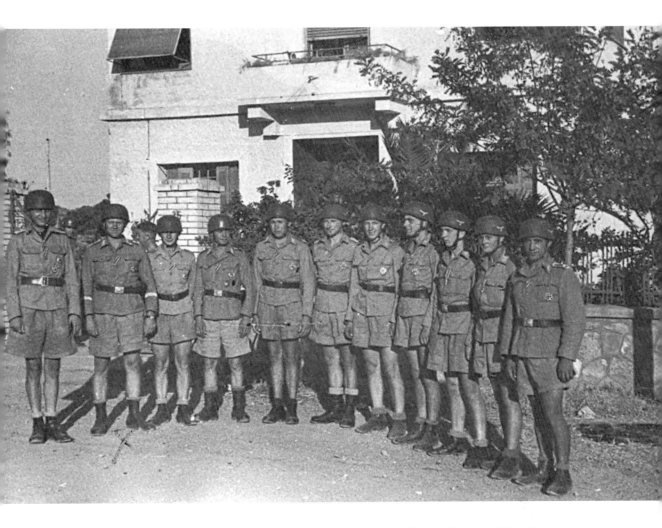

Another group of award winners assemble outside a Cretan house. Plieschen is second from the left in this picture. Considering the fact that the air assault on Rethymno had been a disaster and based on faulty intelligence, these men must have believed themselves incredibly lucky to still be alive. The Germans had launched an assault force of 22,000 men against the island; they suffered 6,500 casualties. Out of this total 3,352 had either been killed or were missing in action. British and Commonwealth forces suffered 3,500 casualties; around 1,700 had been killed and 12,000 had been taken prisoner in addition to 10,000 Greek troops. Operationally, the German airborne forces had done well but everything had been flawed due to the poor intelligence and lack of surprise. Had it not been for the officers and NCOs on the ground the Germans would undoubtedly have lost the battle for the island.

General Kurt Student inspects the unit in this photograph. He had joined the German army in 1910, initially serving as a light infantry officer. He began his pilot training in 1913 and in the period 1916 to 1917 shot down six French aircraft. Student worked hard to maintain the effectiveness of the German air force during the interwar years. In the early 1930s he became head of the *Luftwaffe's* training schools and in July 1938 he became the commander of airborne and air landing troops, taking up the role of the commander of the 7th *Flieger* Division. Student had flown into Crete on 23 May 1941 to personally supervise the battle. His medal ribbons included a wound badge, a *Luftwaffe* combined pilot and observer badge, and a World War One Imperial German Army pilot badge. After the war Student would be charged with war crimes that took place on Crete. He was sentenced to five years, but was released due to ill health after two years. Student was the holder of the Iron Cross, the Knight's Cross of the Iron Cross and a number of other awards.

This is a collection of German and British vehicles, which were photographed in Crete at some point after the capture of the island. Note the Orthodox Greek Church in the background. The 2nd *Fallschirmjäger* Regiment, consisting of the two battalions and the two machine gun companies, remained on Crete only until the beginning of June 1941 and Alfred Sturm remained in command of the regiment until September 1942. Confusingly, the regiment formed the nucleus of the 2nd *Fallschirmjäger* Division, but this was not until February 1943. The regiment, as an independent entity, would spend between October 1941 and July 1942 in Russia and would not return to Germany until that time. We also know that the 2nd *Fallschirmjäger* Regiment had been temporarily based at Plovdiv in Bulgaria in March 1941. This had been its first posting out of Germany since May 1940, when it had been involved in operations in Holland.

This is another photograph of some of the company during Student's visit and inspection. In all likelihood this is at a former British base on the island. Note that many of the buildings to the rear of the men appear to have sustained roof damage. Some of these men may well have been involved in the attack on the Corinth Canal that took place in the early hours of 26 April 1941. It was the only airborne operation that took place during the war without Student's direct knowledge. The 2nd *Fallschirmjäger* Regiment had jumped in to secure the area around Corinth and mop up resistance. The 1st Battalion, under Kroh, had jumped to the north of the bridge; the 2nd Battalion, under Schirmer, had jumped to the south and the 3rd Battalion had dropped a day later, in the afternoon of 27 April.

This is the newly dug grave of Karl Matern, one of the men from the unit that were killed on 20 May 1941. Along with the collection of photographs was a list of the men that had all died on the same day or the day after. All of them had been killed on Vineyard Hill or Bloody Hill. This adds credence to the belief that Sergeant Plieschen had also been dropped in this immediate area. Matern was a *gefreiter*.

This is the grave of another German non-commissioned officer, Gerhard Scheunemann, also of the same machine gun company. He was probably a member of the headquarters unit.

Otto Schmidt's grave is shown in this photograph. This man also fell on 20 May 1941. He was an *oberinspektor*, a senior technical officer, and therefore his primary role would have been predominantly administrative.

Oblt.

Kurt Glanz

✝ 20.5.41

Stab
Fallschirm
MG.Btl.

This is a close-up of the grave of *Oberleutnant* Kurt Glanz. The rank would have been awarded to Glanz as a commissioned officer after five or six years of active duty service. He was the adjutant of the machine gun company and would have worked closely with Major Erich Schulz. A number of the members of the head-quarters unit had been killed on 20 or 21 May. Another member that had worked closely with Schulz and Glanz, Wilhelm Binder, had been killed during the Corinth Canal operation on 26 April 1941.

This is the newly dug grave of *Feldwebel* Heinz Feuerstein, who was killed on 21 May 1941. Although many of these men from the unit were buried almost where they fell, the vast majority of them were later reburied at the German war cemetery near Maleme. The German cemetery that overlooks the airfield itself has 4,000 German troops buried there. A tablet is laid flat on the ground, one for each of the two men. There are also a number of small stone crosses. Incredibly, George Psychoundakis, a Cretan who operated with the SOE throughout the German occupation of the island, worked on tending the graves of the German dead after the war. The German War Graves Commissioner was amazed at the care and attention but surprised that Psychoundakis spoke no German. The Cretan's reply was: 'Well, there's not much opportunity to learn it here. All the Germans I look after are dead.'

George Psychoundakis, also known as the Cretan Runner, died in 2006.

Another grave – this one is close to the sea, and holds the remains of *Gefreiter* Herbert Sutter. The Souda Bay area is dotted with cemeteries. There are 1,509 Second World War graves in the Souda Bay War Cemetery and of these 782 are unidentified. Some 85 km to the east of Souda Bay, on the old coast road at Stavromenos, is a memorial to British, Greek, Australian, and New Zealand and of course Cretan patriots. It consists of paved steps leading up to a terrace where there are two field guns, a pylon and a memorial wall with bronze plaques. The Australian Embassy in Athens takes care of its upkeep.

Chapter Three

Russia

After the massive losses on Crete the 7th *Flieger* Division made its way back to Germany for much needed rest, refitting and reinforcement. The Germans launched Operation *Barbarossa* in June 1941, but without the use of the *Fallschirmjäger*. However, their deployment to Russia was imminent. By the end of September 1941 parts of the division were already being sent east; this time to operate as conventional infantry.

The 1st Regiment's 1st and 3rd Battalions, along with the 2nd Battalion of the *Sturm* Regiment, were sent for duty on the Leningrad front. It was a problematic part of the front for both the Germans and the Russians. The 2nd and 3rd Battalion of the 3rd Regiment arrived on 1 October and the division's headquarters arrived in the mid-October. Other units began trickling into the region.

The Russians were desperate to break through to Leningrad to raise the siege. The fighting was extremely heavy and by December 1941 the casualties had been so high that the *Fallschirmjäger* in the Leningrad area was pulled out and returned to Germany.

The 2nd Regiment, of which Plieschen was attached, had been held back as a reserve. They were sent in November 1941 to join Army Group South, fighting in the Ukraine. The winter had put a stop to the German advances and they were now on the defensive. The Russians were launching attack after attack in the region. Army Group South found itself spread out across the whole of the Ukraine. The 2nd Regiment became part of an ad hoc battle group, or *Kampfgruppe*, along with the 4th Battalion of the assault regiment, a company from the anti-tank battalion and, of course, the machine gun companies. Sturm commanded the unit himself and they were ordered to defend a sector that ran along the River Mius, close to the town of Charzysk. They would defend this whole area throughout the winter of 1941 and into the early months of 1942.

In March 1942 the 2nd Regiment was moved from the south to the Volkhov area of the front. This was where the 1st Regiment had fought in the previous year. The regiment came under the command of the 21st Infantry Division. It was a very bad time for them to be moving to the area; the Russians were regrouping and about to launch a massive offensive aimed at breaking through to Leningrad.

What must have been a rude awakening for the *Fallschirmjäger*, having suffered a harsh environment in Crete only to be followed by the opposite in weather conditions in snow-covered Russia. This is probably around the Stalino area, which is now in the Ukraine. Field Marshal von Rundstedt was tasked with the capture of the Ukraine and the Crimea, as his part of Operation *Barbarossa*. The forty-six and a half divisions under his command attacked on a front of 800 miles, beginning at 0100 hours on 22 June 1941. By the time the *Fallschirmjäger* units began to arrive in the region Army Group South had already overrun Kiev, Odessa, and Kharkov. The *Fallschirmjäger*, operating as infantrymen, bore the brunt of the fighting. It was they that secured ground and then held it.

An unidentified Russian Orthodox Church is shown in this photograph. At Kiev alone the Germans had taken 665,000 prisoners. However, the fighting around this part of the Ukraine was extremely bitter. Under the command of Sturm the unit fought around Stalino (Donetsk). This city was virtually destroyed during the war. In 1941 it had had a population of over 500,000; only 175,000 remained after the war. We also know that the unit fought at Woroschilkovka (Woroschilowgrad), Ivanovka and Petropawlowsk. We also know that a second *Kampfgruppe*, under Meindl, was formed from the 1st Battalion of the 2nd Regiment. It included the assault units, under Major Walter Koch. This force was sent to cover the town of Vyasma, some ninety-five miles to the east of Smolensk.

This is an intriguing photograph of the paratroopers, presumably in a period of thaw in Russia. This photograph may have been out of sequence in the photograph album, as it is certain that by the time the 2nd Regiment arrived in Russia there was already heavy snow. *Kampfgruppe* Meindl was joined by scattered groups of *Wehrmacht* and SS units that had suffered heavy casualties. It is not clear precisely where the machine gun company was deployed at this time; it either remained with the bulk of the 2nd Regiment, on the River Mius close to Yuknov, or was part of *Kampfgruppe* Meindl. A series of battles developed around this area, as the Russians launched a major counteroffensive. For several weeks the paratroopers held back the onslaught, being reinforced by *Kampfgruppe* Meindl. Ultimately the Soviet high command halted the attacks due to the enormous casualties.

In all likelihood this is a photograph of the unit being transferred north to the Volkhov area in either March or April 1942. Here they would fight in the same area near Leningrad where the 1st Regiment had been in action in 1941. The 2nd Regiment was to be deployed around the small town of Lipovka. What is confusing about the deployment of the particular units is that there are references to the 2nd Company of the *Fallschirmjäger* machine gun battalion in action around the Volkhov front, near Leningrad in September and October 1941. It was on the River Neva that the *Fallschirmjäger* units saw their first action on the eastern front. The Russians had launched a series of attacks aiming to penetrate the weakly held German line around Leningrad. The plan was that the Russian armies would break through the German defences and link up with forces pushing from out of the city. It was here, on the River Neva, that elements of the 2nd Battalion of the assault regiment, backed up by the 2nd Company of the *Fallschirmjäger* machine gun battalion, held back huge attacks by Russian tanks and massed infantry. They took massive casualties and on 7 October they were pulled out of the line and redeployed on another sector of the River Neva where a new Russian attack was developing.

This photograph suggests that the unit is in transit in relatively good weather. Again, this might be a symptom of the fact that the photographs in the album are out of order. What is clear, however, is that the 2nd and 3rd Battalions of the 3rd Regiment, under Heidrich, had reached the Leningrad front at the beginning of October 1941. They were tasked with the job of covering the flanks of the assault regiment, which was counter-attacking a number of Russian bridgeheads. We also know that two companies of the *Fallschirmjäger* Pioneer Battalion, under Major Liebach, arrived around mid-October and they were thrown straight into action on the western side of the River Neva. They operated in woodland near Sinyavino. This was some 58 km to the east of Leningrad and was a relatively new town that had only been established in 1930. Having said that, this was the place where the Russians had decided to concentrate the bulk of their reserves in their build up to another breakthrough towards Leningrad. The engineers took possession of the woods and destroyed a large number of tanks with grenades and mines. The Russians tried everything to dislodge them but ultimately, on 16 November, they were pulled out and sent back to Germany for rest and refitting.

The majority of the men in this photograph are wearing the standard NCO and enlisted men's side cap. On the side of the rolling stock from which the German soldier is dispensing rations it says *Deutsche Reichsbahn*. This simply means German Reich Railway. It was reorganised in 1937 and since the 1920s had been 100 per cent owned by the German state.

Christmas in a bombproof bunker is shown in this photograph. Note that the clothing of the *Fallschirmjäger* is pegged out along the rear wall to dry and that it is somewhat different from the clothing that was worn by the *Fallschirmjäger* back in Crete in May 1941. The camouflage equipment appears to be the reversible winter parka, which had a splinter pattern on one side and was grey on the other side. *Fallschirmjäger* in Russia would wear a mixture of *Luftwaffe* and *Gebirgsjäger* clothing. Some would wear white ski suits. In 1942 many of the *Fallschirmjäger* were issued with single-breasted combat jackets, known as *kampfjacke*, which were a mixture of rayon and cotton in splinter camouflage. These were the same as those issued to *Luftwaffe* field divisions. The only insignia that were worn on these smocks and combat jackets were the breast eagle of the *Luftwaffe* and the cloth rank badges on the sleeves. The combat trousers were relatively loose fitting; they aimed to be comfortable and to be easy to move around in. They were fastened at the ankle by tape and had two side and two hip pockets and a fob pocket under the waistband. They could be held up either with a belt or braces. On the outside of each of the knees was a vent where a rectangular canvas pad filled with kapok could be inserted to protect the knees. This did not work that well and for combat jumps external pads were strapped on.

This intriguing photograph shows two First World War vintage tanks outside a large Russian building. These tanks may well now be in the Kharkov Historical Museum in the Ukraine. These were tanks that were delivered by Britain to Russia after the First World War. They were sent in support of the anti-Communist forces during the Russian civil war and subsequently captured and used as monuments. At the time it is believed that these tanks were on display in Smolensk, which makes a great deal of sense since the machine gun company was in this area over the winter of 1941 to 1942. There are a number of these tanks in Russia, also at the Tank Museum at Kubinka. Here they have a British Mark V, which was captured by the Red Army in April 1920.

Three of the men from the unit are seen here in fatigue dress, with lined boots. Note that the man on the right has his Iron Cross on his chest. Despite contradictory information, the 2nd *Fallschirmjäger* MG Battalion 7, of which Plieschen was a member, appears to have been simultaneously deployed both around the River Neva sector of the Leningrad front and in the Ukraine. Elements of the unit are listed as having entrained for the Leningrad front, arriving there in October 1941. The units in this area suffered 1,000 dead or missing and 2,000 wounded. Likewise, elements of the same machine gun unit were operating in the Ukraine under Sturm and they held the line around Stalino throughout January 1942. This is further confused by the fact that additional parachute troops, under Meindl, were also operating in the same area. We can only assume that Plieschen was part of this Ukrainian operation, as his photographs seem to suggest that he was in the Smolensk area.

Fallschirmjäger in white coveralls are about to leave for a patrol on the Russian front. The personal weapons used by the *Fallschirmjäger* were fairly standard, except that they had the specially designed FG42 assault rifle. They would also tend to have a higher ratio of automatic weapons, such as the MP40. The *Fallschirmjäger* operating around Lipovka, near Leningrad, faced stiff opposition on 9 May 1942, when they came under attack from Russian aircraft aiming to soften up their positions before determined mass attacks by Russian infantry. After withstanding the attacks for four days the paratrooper units were reinforced by tanks and self-propelled guns. The line was held and, in fact, the Russians were forced back to their start line. On 14 May the 2nd Regiment was ordered to counterattack Russian positions to the east of Lipovka. Sturm flew to Berlin when he received the order from the 21st Infantry Division. His protests were ignored and the attack went in under a cover of artillery fire. As the attack progressed the Russians began to envelop them and the paratroopers were forced to withdraw, taking as many of their wounded with them as possible. By the evening of 14 May they were back at their start line, having achieved nothing.

Paratroopers look over a collection of captured Russian tanks in this photograph. The tank in the foreground is a Russian BT7. Incredibly, one of these tanks was salvaged from the Neva River on 18 June 2007. This was a light tank that was designed in the 1930s. It had rubber-coated wheels and an engine based on American designs. It fired 45-mm ammunition and held 132 shells. The command version was known as the BT5 and this one had a radio. The BT7 weighed 13.8 tons, had a three-man crew, a range of 500 km and could reach speeds of up to 72 km/hour. A large number of Russian tanks have been found in the Neva River and many of them are now kept at the Nevskij Bridgehead Museum.

Undoubtedly, this is a posed shot but here we can clearly see a *Fallschirmjäger* anti-aircraft crew in action, hunting the skies for approaching Russian aircraft. During the rest of May 1942 the survivors of the 2nd Regiment tended to only be used on reconnaissance duties. The bulk of the regiment was sent home to Germany in June 1942, although some elements of the 2nd Regiment remained behind in Russia until the July. By the summer of 1942 they had exchanged the nightmare of the Russian front for the relative peace of Normandy in France. It was around this time that the 2nd Regiment was transferred to duties in North Africa. As for the rest of the division, now consisting of six battalions, they would be transferred back to the Russian front. There were plans for an air drop in southern Russia in order to capture oilfields, but this was cancelled in September 1942. Instead, the 7th Airborne, comprising the 1st, 3rd and 4th Regiments, plus support units, were in Smolensk. Here they would defend a fifty-six-mile sector to the north of the Smolensk to Vitebsk Highway.

Another posed photograph of members of the unit in their full winter gear. Note that they are all heavily armed with ammunition bandoliers and a variety of rifles and automatic weapons. The division, now operating around Smolensk, was positioned on the part of the sector that was expected to receive the brunt of an upcoming Russian offensive. They were tasked with carrying out long-range probing missions to disrupt the Russian build up. This took place throughout October 1942; largely as a result of their aggressive action the Russians abandoned their attempt to launch an offensive against this stretch of the sector and chose a weaker one instead. The *Fallschirmjäger* of the 7th Airborne then had the rest of the year and the beginning of 1943 as a relatively inactive participant on the eastern front. This gave them an opportunity to reorganise, refit and reinforce.

This is a dramatic photograph, as a shell explodes amongst buildings beside a snowbound road. By March 1943 the 7th Airborne was due to be relieved but this coincided with a major offensive launched by the Russians against their sector. At Lushki the *Fallschirmjäger* held a hill against determined Russian attacks. The men defending the hill were members of the 3rd Battalion of the 4th Regiment. They were reinforced by the 3rd Battalion of the 3rd Regiment and over a period between 20 and 27 March these two battalions held back two complete Soviet divisions. By the end of March the situation had stabilised. The division, now under the command of General Richard Heidrich, was transferred to the west and sent to southern France.

Here an NCO and officer stand beside a log-built shelter on the Russian front during the winter of 1941 to 1942. If we assume that the 2nd *Fallschirmjäger* Regiment was indeed withdrawn earlier than the events in late 1942 and that Plieschen was one of these men, then he would ultimately become a part of the newly formed 2nd *Fallschirmjäger* Division, under Ramcke. In fact, the 2nd *Fallschirmjäger* Regiment became the nucleus of this new division. Ramcke had been on Crete and in 1942 his *Fallschirmjäger Brigade Afrika* had been sent to North Africa. By 1943 he had taken command of the 2nd *Fallschirmjäger* Division. It was deployed to Italy and was there to ensure that the Italians remained loyal to Germany. He took part in Operation *Achse* in September 1943 when Italy signed an armistice with the Allies. It was his division that secured Rome. Shortly after this Ramcke was wounded after his car was forced off the road after being attacked by an Allied aircraft.

Fallschirmjäger are resting in their dugout during the winter of 1941 to 1942 in this photograph. Note the wide variety of different clothes and variants of uniforms worn by the men. By early 1944 the 2nd *Fallschirmjäger* Regiment was back on the eastern front. Ultimately, the division was withdrawn and sent for refitting near Cologne. Once the Allies had landed in Normandy in June 1944 the 2nd *Fallschirmjäger* Division was despatched to Brittany and here it became responsible for the defence of Brest. Ramcke was one of only twenty-seven Germans to receive the Knight's Cross with Swords, Oak Leaves and Diamonds.

This photograph shows a mass grave of German troops. Underneath the swastika can be seen '1939', which strongly suggests that this photograph may well have been taken in Poland rather than in Russia. This is somewhat surprising if indeed it has any link at all with the parachute troops. Certainly, the 2nd *Fallschirmjäger* Regiment played no part in the attack on Poland in 1939 and neither did any other paratrooper unit. This may simply be a mass grave that Plieschen happened upon at some point, perhaps during a rest period from the front line two years later.

The centre grave at the front is one of a *feldwebel* of the *Fallschirmjäger* machine gun company to which Plieschen belonged. The date of death is given as 1 January 1942. Alongside are other men from different units, who died in and around the same time as this paratrooper. The grave to the left is that of a *feldwebel* that belonged to the 2nd Panzer Division and from the description he was in an anti-aircraft unit and died a day after the paratrooper. It is also interesting to consider the relatively young age of the fallen *Fallschirmjäger*; he was just twenty-three.

This is a more permanent tribute to the same man as in the previous photograph who was killed on 1 January 1942. He was Josef-Heinz Hollodzey. The inscription simply reads that he was a member of the machine gun battalion. This *feldwebel* was born on 25 May 1919 and he would have been twenty-one when he was air dropped onto Crete.

This is the first of a series of three photographs that were presumably taken around the same time as the burials of the men from the machine gun unit that were killed over the Christmas period 1941 to 1942. Despite the conditions the men are wearing their best uniforms and their decorations.

Members of the unit line up to salute their fallen comrades. Note that the majority of the men are wearing their sidearms and that prudently most have gloves. There is also a mix of footwear, although fur-lined boots predominate. Note also that there are several members of this group that are Iron Cross winners.

The senior officers of the unit are shown saluting the fallen members of the company in this photograph. It is difficult to be clear as to whether or not Plieschen survived the war since these photographs and the two at the end of the photograph album appear to show him later with a moustache. It is not clear precisely when these last photographs were taken. What we do know is that the 2nd *Fallschirmjäger* Division became trapped in Brest following Operation *Cobra*, which was launched in late July 1944. Ramcke's men fell back on Brest, turning it into a strong point in an attempt to hold onto this vital port. With him were around 35,000 German troops. They stubbornly held onto Brest between 11 August and 19 September. On 19 September he finally surrendered and the men were taken into captivity.

This is an interesting photograph of a much older-looking Plieschen. He has clearly suffered from the rigours and dangers of the eastern front and this may well be a photograph of him heading west in the summer of 1942. The fighting was by no means over for Plieschen and his unit. Additional tours of duty on the eastern front around Kirovograd in January 1944 were yet to come, as indeed were operations on the eastern front until May of 1944. As for the division itself, the vast majority of them had surrendered in September 1944 to the Americans. A handful of the division managed to withdraw towards Germany. The 2nd Parachute Regiment itself was reconstituted the same month in Holland and, along with the 7th and 23rd Parachute Regiments, a new 2nd Parachute Division was created. It would fight on until it finally surrendered in the Ruhr pocket in April 1945.

Plieschen displays his accumulation of decorations for valour and service during the early stages of the Second World War here. His cuffs display a band that designates him as one of the men involved in the Crete operation and his Iron Cross can be clearly seen. Once the 2nd *Fallschirmjäger* Regiment became subsumed as part of the 2nd *Fallschirmjäger* Division, it is difficult to know precisely where Plieschen served. Elements of the 2nd *Fallschirmjäger* Regiment were on Leros in late 1943 and in November 1943 part of the division remained in Italy to form part of the 4th *Fallschirmjäger* Division. This means that it is incredibly difficult to trace the movements of the machine gun company, let alone those of Plieschen. There is no information to support whether or not he was transferred, having been promoted, or whether he remained with the machine gun unit. It would be incredible to believe that any of the men could have survived over four years of continuous combat action with only short periods of rest. In many respects the *Fallschirmjäger* had been transformed from a primary strike weapon in the armoury of the German war machine to become Hitler's fire brigade, as they were nicknamed.

Bibliography

Beevor, Antony, *Crete*, John Murray, 2005

Kurtz, Robert, *German Paratroops*, Schiffer Publishing, 2004

McNab, Chris, *German Paratroopers*, Aurum Press, 2000

Nasse, Jean-Wves, *Fallschirmjäger in Crete*, Historie and Collections, 2002

Peters, Klaus, *A Pictorial History of Fallschirmjäger Regiment 3*, R James, 1992

Psychoundakis, George, *The Cretan Runner*, John Murray, 1955

Saunders, Tim, *Crete: The Airborne Invasion 1941*, Pen & Sword, 2008

Stewart, I McD G, *The Struggle for Crete*, Oxford University Press, 1966